FINANCIAL FREEDOM

FINANCIAL FREEDOM

LUNA EMBER

CONTENTS

First Printing, 2024

CHAPTER 1

Introduction to Financial Freedom

Financial Freedom: Strategies for Building Wealth and Achieving Independence

If you're interested in achieving wealth, being rich is not the same as being financially free. Being rich only means that you have a lot of money. If you are rich and have to work all the time, you are not financially free. On the other hand, if you are financially free, you have the ability to be rich or not, because your money is working for you. That's the whole point of financial freedom: having enough money to have the options you want, without having to work for it. If your money is working for you, and not vice versa, it's a good indication that you are already financially free.

The most important factor to consider is whether you want to be financially free and to what extent. Many people simply never try to achieve financial freedom because they don't really want it. Some people like their jobs more than their recreational time and so they work as much as possible. Some people know that if they stay in their jobs long enough, they won't be able to leave, even after they retire. A lifetime of high income spending without saving won't let them achieve the financial independence in retirement since all of their income stops once they actually reach financial independence. And remember, if you never try to achieve financial freedom, you're far less likely to be able to have fun with the necessary micromanagement of your money once you get there. The earlier in life that you start, the earlier that you can retire and begin to enjoy the benefits of financial freedom.

Defining Financial Freedom

No particular level defines wealth. Your own definition is related to where you are in life and what you aspire to acquire. The less money you feel is necessary for each of the stages in your life, the closer you are to the freedom you seek. It takes discipline, belief in yourself, and an understanding of your strengths and weaknesses to act on the response. The path to financial independence necessarily isn't linear either. You will face tests of character on multiple levels and personal situations will catch you unaware. The effort takes time. It calls on you to consider the choices you make. When you begin to view the world from this perspective, a broader view of the world emerges, as well. Knowing yourself respected societal templates become practice exercises, reasonable outcomes that a culture unto finance should question for its relevance and value to those who subscribe to it. Focus in the riches society and exchange in commerce is a side order to your exploring the world and all its glory.

When you reach the juncture of financial independence, choices in your life that you would normally occupy many of your thoughts tend to fall away. You will be free to choose instead of having a lifestyle determined by a career. Becoming rich is not the answer. It requires striving for freedom. It means enjoying your accomplishments, being brave, and courageously moving only in the direction of your goals regardless of what others might say or think. The quest for financial freedom's greatest benefit is that it allows you to experience the world with a sense of means and wonder and your place within it.

Importance and Benefits

There are many benefits of being able to possess or be close to financial freedom. Such a position enables us to be increasingly self-sufficient and less reliant on others. The richer we are, the less ability others have to control our lives. We are able to make decisions and take risks without fearing the potential financial implications. If things don't work out, then we can generally afford to try again. If things do work as anticipated, then we continue to reap the financial rewards. As our security and wealth build up, we can concentrate on improving our lifestyle and happiness. There is less pressure for us to conform to benchmarks or the standards imposed by other people, groups, or society.

The importance of attaining financial freedom cannot be overemphasized, especially in a world characterized by so much uncertainty. The desire to achieve success in life is universal and has been found to be the primary motivation for most of our actions, whether at personal, family, or community levels. Understanding the concept of financial freedom or wealth is an important measure of our personal success and independence. Financial freedom can be defined as the ability to finance one's desired lifestyle without the need to be employed or work. This means that we can become our own bosses, make decisions for our lives without caring for financial implications. Rather than being crippled by financial worries and concerns, we are free to give and share of ourselves because we have eliminated or minimized the fear and anxiety from our lives. However we define wealth, it is generally perceived as a measure of our happiness.

CHAPTER 2

Understanding Wealth Building

Now that I have that out of the way, let's look at some of these principles: There is no secret to building wealth - it is a process that can be learned, like anything else. The first part of that learning process is to first understand the concept of money. Money is just a piece of paper that has some writing or some marks on it. It only has whatever value we place on it. But that is not really money. That is just the physical manifestation of a much larger concept of money, which is precisely this: "The result of a specific set of activities, transactions, selling goods, or performing specific investments that when sold, results in the ability to spend without going broke." Think of that. In business, what makes a company a going concern? It is the fact that the company owns a few things that other people want to buy. Not something, but something that other people want to buy. That is the very definition of anything that has value.

Notice that I use the word "possibility." It is important to know this because financial freedom is not something that just happens - it is not theory. It occurs as the result of specific processes that take place. This plays on the principle that everything happens for a reason. So does financial freedom. If wealth building concepts and principles are learned, then practiced in a specific way, then financial freedom becomes a possibility. This may vary from a possibility to an eventuality, but it is only an issue of being willing then acting out the processes that bring it into being. Without both the willingness and taking the specific actions, financial freedom will not happen.

Key Concepts and Principles

Therefore, financial freedom means that you have reached a level of wealth that allows you to be more selective about where, when, and with whom you spend your time. At this level of wealth, you are able to fully exploit the person success and find out what you're really capable of. This is the reason that, whatever business you're in or whatever the economy is doing, while many might worry about the ups and downs of the markets, or of the world, the rich just continue focusing on what they can do. The rich are not focused on markets, the economy, or tough luck, but keep their focus on themselves to get ahead in the game no matter what be happening in the world around them. They are focused on their personal "road to wealth."

What this means can manifest itself in all sorts of ways. For example, you might want to visit your kids/grandkids and the managing director of your company invites you to a business trip. You think, "This will be the opportunity, I can kill two birds with one stone!" Then you realize that because you cannot count on the his boss, the executive director, to handle most of your responsibilities while you're away, your day is filled with tasks and activities like visiting clients, working on proposals, and doing follow-up work. Possible work challenges and priorities are getting in the way of the visit.

Let's start by establishing some key concepts and principles. The first concept we want to address is the idea of financial freedom itself. What is financial freedom? The concept is rather self-explanatory - freedom of choice that derives from your finances. What this means is that you are able to do what you want, when you want, where you want, and with whom you want, without having to worry about debt, sacrifice your lifestyle or take up more work.

Types of Assets

Fixed-Income Investments. The first requirement of an investor should be the return of his money. The second is a good return on his money. Historically, the best investments in these areas have been fixed-income investments. In other words, fixed-income investing is one way to lend your money in return for a specific promise to receive all of it back along with interest at regularly scheduled intervals. Interest can be paid at a fixed rate or follow a fixed formula. In most cases, fixed-income investments do not have the capital appreciation potential of other investments. However, they are often less risky. Examples of fixed-income investments include U.S. Savings Bonds, U.S. Treasury Notes, corporate bonds, and municipal bonds.

Income Stocks. Many companies pay shareholders dividends, or cash payments, often four times a year. These are called income stocks. Shareholders usually are free to spend the money as they see fit. In the past, however, most shareholders chose to reinvest their dividend income by buying additional shares of stock.

Stocks. When you invest in stock, you buy a tiny share of ownership in a particular company. Most popular stocks are those of large, well-known corporations, such as Microsoft, General Motors, and General Electric. These are called blue chip stocks. Because the futures of this country's largest companies can significantly affect the overall economy, blue chip stocks are a major investment area.

When financial experts refer to an asset, they are often talking about a category of investments. These investments share certain characteristics. Here are some of the most common types:

CHAPTER 3

Budgeting and Saving

The first step is to define your budgeting time period. Is it annual, quarterly, monthly, biweekly? You may be disappointed to learn that it is necessary to budget for holidays, gifts, and vacations. You do that by setting aside a little something each payday to help finance these events. I can assure you that a solid, balanced budget is the only road to end the paycheck-to-paycheck cycle. You will be astounded at how much money is going down the drain without you ever knowing it. It is not so much that you will be confronted with bills or expenses that you cannot meet, it is the realization that you lived well beyond your means for such a long time because of unplanned and unnecessary expenses. Only through this process can you really analyze and understand the full cost of ownership of anything or accept the fact that you really cannot afford a new luxury automobile.

Budgeting is the most important tool for providing financial security. It is a planning process that helps you manage expenses and provides a mechanism to identify sources and uses of funds for a specified period of time. You will find that tracking your income and expenses and analyzing your results empower you to maximize your discretionary income. The framework of personal financial planning in this chapter provides the groundwork for establishing a budget plan. Since the rates of return are so low on short-term investments, often less than 2 percent, it is difficult to build much of an emergency reserve without first getting control of your bills and out-of-pocket expenses.

Creating a Budget Plan

What's the solution? Operate with a budget. This is your blueprint for the way you are going to spend your money in the future. The process involves taking a look at what you are earning now and making a statement of your projected income for the period ahead. Next, you must make estimates of what each of your costs for the period ahead is likely to be. Once you have actually done the spending, compare the evaluations to the actual expenses. In addition, carry over the spending variances you may have discovered to your next spending plan. By keeping close tabs on your plan, you'll be able to tell when your costs are zooming taller than your income trees. When that happens, you know you'll have to cut back, grow more money, work for more money, or pay for your spending out of capital assets. Keep money from playing tricks on you by regularly working a spending plan.

Whether you earn a high income or a low one, you can still have plenty of money to spend and be a poor money manager. They get in debt. They have to pay large interest charges. And, as a result, they have to spend lots of time earning the money to cover all their costs. If they could learn to run their money on less, they would have a larger percentage of their income free to invest in a long-term plan to achieve their dreams.

Effective Saving Strategies

The first step towards wealth is learning to save. You cannot grow wealth if you do not save. There are a few strategies you can put in place to achieve effective saving.

Set saving goals: Saving is very hard initially because you learn to live on what is left after you save. Many good upbringings require you to save first before you spend. If you are not used to living on less initially, set savings targets each month. For example, plan to save 10% of your income or $1,000 each month. If you do not have a strategy on how much you should save, you end up spending everything you earn and will never achieve financial freedom.

Live within your means: You cannot expect to achieve financial freedom if you live beyond your means. We live in a very materialistic society, but we need to learn to live on less to save more. Materialistic consumption will just set you back in your quest to achieve financial freedom. Allocate a certain amount for discretionary income based on what is left after your basic, discretionary, and variable expenses are accounted for. Furthermore, saving can help you to manage unplanned expenses and also provide for your future.

Pay yourself first: After income has been earned and collected, take a percentage out and save it for yourself. This will make it easy for you to learn to live on what is left. If you pay yourself first, you will be surprised at how disciplined you can become with the money that is left after everything has been accounted for. If you take out savings last, you are less likely to have any leftover. You may even incur additional expenses from which to make up the shortfall. The main contention for saving last is that you never manage to save anything and everything you have earned evaporates. I believe an effective saving plan must involve this principle. For paycheck earners, it is recommended that you have it taken right from your paycheck and transferred into a savings or investment account. This would make it systematic and behavioral, and each month you will learn to live on less, that is until your next raise.

Save bonuses and windfalls: Bonuses and windfalls provide a good opportunity to boost your savings. I suggest 100% be immediately invested. However, if that is unrealistic, at least make some kind of investment. Bonuses and windfalls come up infrequently. However, if you become a consistent saver, at least you will have the opportunity to take advantage when they do. It does not matter when they occur as long as your plan is in place. Some other retirement strategies include living off your income and saving your bonus.

Save on taxes: One of the benefits of making a contribution to a retirement savings account is that the amount of the contribution is deducted from your income. For example, money that is contributed into a 401(k) is free from federal, and in some cases, state and local income taxes. Using this strategy will reduce the amount of federal income tax you owe. I suggest you put the tax savings from your retirement plan directly into a personal savings or investment account.

CHAPTER 4

Investing for the Future

Stocks, bonds, and mutual funds are meant to be long-term investments. Retirement account savings are meant to be used only in your retirement years. This does not mean you cannot withdraw money earlier or stop contributing to any of these investment options in times of need. You simply have to account for the consequences which could result in losing some of the money you earned on your investment. Before deciding what investment is right for you, learn and talk to professionals about investing your money for the future. Look for the investment that is right for you in terms of your future and what you are comfortable with. Our savings for investing were supposed to last throughout our living years. We built up more money than we originally thought possible. All so we could feed and house our family and live comfortably on what we saved and earned by investing.

When you build up your six-month cushion of money for your living expenses, your emergency fund, and an investment cushion to get you started, you must consider how to place some of your money to build more money. Putting some of your money into investments allows it to grow. We saved money for a long time while living with loved ones so that money could work for us in the future by making more money. To make your money work and grow, explore your investment options. Research stocks, bonds, and mutual funds as well as retirement accounts. Set goals for investing where you want your money to be in a few years and into your retirement. Find what you are comfortable with because investing does involve taking some risk with your original investment.

Types of Investments

Growth investments produce the best long-term returns. They are stocks or funds whose value is best measured by their price-earnings (P/E) ratios. We would use price-to-sales ratios for utility stocks or price to asset values or other ratios to compare other types of investments. We use the P/E for growth because it directly measures the relationship between the amount of earnings capital is generating and the price we are paying for those earnings. In other words, companies that have high, growing and sustainable rates of earnings growth deserve higher P/Es than companies without a history of such rates of earnings growth. For example, if you have two companies, one that is growing its earnings at 10% a year and the other that is growing its earnings at 5% a year, but both are selling at 20 times earnings, the first company would be a traditional growth stock. The second would be just a high P/E stock.

Investments can be classified in a number of ways. The traditional method of grouping them was by asset class—whether they were stocks or bonds or real estate, for example. However, this type of classification is not entirely useful to us, especially if we are trying to build wealth rapidly and maximize income. We will be grouping investments by how they produce returns. For example, to achieve certain financial goals, we need to have capital appreciation. To achieve some traditional wealth-building goals, we need a high level of return, commonly in the form of higher current income. You should have a mix of all these investment types as well as varying by quality. Different investments have different purposes in our portfolios. In this chapter, we will discuss their different purposes and how to construct a portfolio that includes them all.

Risk Management

In order to manage risk, you should know the risks that you can expect your portfolio to face. Being knowledgeable about a particular risk allows you to decide whether you would or would not like to accept this risk, as opposed to being dumbstruck and unknowingly facing it. You should be aware of three key strategies of risk management: diversification, asset allocation, and prudent investment selection. A properly diversified portfolio can avoid problems we discussed in selecting the wrong stock or bond at the wrong time. Even if you avoided company-specific risk by investing in a well-known, seemingly safe firm, there are external events which can destroy the firm, and with it, the value of your investment. In this era of mega-mergers, no company is beyond the reach of being bought in a hostile takeover. So unless you are willing to actively manage investments in individual companies and are aware of the interest of others in destroying it, you should spread your money across several companies and industries. Diversification is important in bonds, too. Industry-specific policies, economic trends, and events will be poorly matched to the liability of individual firms. To avoid a lack of diversification in any one industry or sector, carefully consider whether you should purchase Treasury notes or bonds, which make good investment-grade corporate bonds. Spreading your capital around to the appropriate investment vehicles in the appropriate place is what we call asset allocation. Diversify your capital not only across different types of investments but place it in different asset classes in different geographic regions and, as appropriate, different currencies and time frames. Prudent investment selection is the process of applying your asset allocation strategies and then filtering it down to individual securities. You should always try to select investments that will grow while placing a minimum amount of capital on the line. Furthermore, you should attempt to take into account all the uncertainties that will affect the value of the security from the day you take ownership until the day you sell it. By thoughtfully considering the risks to capital, it is less likely that your financial dreams will falter into a nightmare. You can "supplement" active management with some idea and money management of your own. The important factor, then, becomes knowing the difference between luck and skill. If you are with great financial advisors, any short-term underperformance or a strategic divergence could be rejected. Even if the complex had many outcomes, note that when outcomes vary, some money management must beat the average. Keep a journal of what should be outstanding investments and why. Then you should compare these investments and suggest continuously proving yourself. He may even give you better ideas and better service. As you manage, you might even reduce fees when you really do beat the mirror.

Any financial plan you and, ultimately, your financial advisor develop should consider the two fundamental factors which define any investment strategy: risk and return. At their most basic level, investments allow you the possibility of earning a return on saved capital. The trade-off for having such an opportunity, though, is that you are required to assume the risk of market losses. The only way one can completely avoid risk is to stay out of the market. But by avoiding the market, you also forgo the opportunity to earn returns. Only by understanding the extent to which risk can be managed will there be any money around to earn returns. It conflicts directly with our human nature, but we must undertake some level of risk and trust the market and our planning to turn capital into future values.

CHAPTER 5

Debt Management and Reduction

When in the ruts of debt, work to get out. The old fox knows you are trapped in your home when he can make you financially unhappy (increase your monthly payments so that you operate at a loss). He also knows that when you operate at a loss for a few months you will go bankrupt, which is fatal to your financial status. Knowing this, he is content with only six or seven percent return on his investment, and he equates your home with his individual financial excellence. You can see he will not release you so that you might become more equal to him. He won't even give you the money he would have had at a higher return to increase your investments because he doesn't want you in any position where you might supplant him! He wants to work you and your spouse to death so that he makes enough profit to hire family members on a permanent basis. A word to the wise, get out if you can't get out. Beede, one year, and all of a sudden I'm advised that in Beede retirement he accumulated enough that they said Beede could stand an annual loss of thirty-five thousand dollars and live until he was Meg's age. After a three-minute soak, I said "15.5%". Do not let the fox get you in the rut of debt.

Debt management simply means the intelligent use of debt to help you improve and broaden your financial situation. Someone asked me yesterday if there was such a thing as good debt. Of course, I replied. Debt that decreases in value. In other words, if you borrow money at seven percent interest, what can you do with it that will return seventeen percent? If you can do something with it that will return twenty percent, do you see the benefit of borrowing money? On the other hand, dollars at fifteen percent on credit card interest does not pass the good debt test. For those of you who understand the theory of debt management and are not yet doing it, wake up! The wealth you build can probably be built faster because you are using other people's money. It really is fun to let money make money. If you aren't doing it, sex yourself up to learn how or get out of debt where you won't be able to play in the financial freedom game.

Understanding Debt

It is also wise to remember the biblical fact that "Debt is Servitude." It is truly the millstone that weighs too heavily around the neck of the borrower. Greed has been said to be the constant desire to achieve a higher level of consumption. This desire has proven to be most costly, as the vast majority of individual investors have too often and consistently sought the greatest gains with the least amount of risk. Control your greed and do not let it control you.

Interest is the cost of debt and is traditionally calculated at an annual rate, expressed as an APR, and then divided by 365. The result is multiplied by the ending balance, which will give you the annual interest cost. Interest is then added to the original balance or principal amount, and the borrower pays interest on both the principal and on the interest. However, the full result is 8%. Interest is received by the investor. In conclusion, remember that interest is always tied to debt, and the greater the levels of debt used by a borrower, the higher the interest costs and the greater the overall risk to the borrower.

Strategies for Paying Off Debt

The debt snowball method works on the premise that you pay off the loan with the lowest balance first. The remaining money is then applied to the next lowest loan. Continue this process, and you are eventually left with the home mortgage. In the event of a tie, pay off the highest interest rate first, starting with the highest balance. Approach the lowest total balance in all credit cards first, if both, or all, of the following conditions exist: They have a balance with an interest that is still in the promotional period and they will reset shortly. If tied, the next lowest total due in a loan and/or credit card would exceed the promotional period.

This strategy is simple, but requires discipline and some belt-tightening. First, develop a list of the debts you have, specifically home mortgage, auto loans, and credit card balances. When considering paying off variable-cost loans such as the mortgage, auto, and credit cards, you are going to use a debt snowball approach. The only non-variable cost loan is the home mortgage. For the mortgage loan, you pay off the 30-year loan before you move to your other milestones associated with financial freedom. The next step is to determine the order in which you will pay off all debts, as you will pay minimum payments on all other debt spread throughout the other milestones, and nothing more.

CHAPTER 6

Income Generation and Passive Income

Social security payments will become necessary when you are older if your income cannot be replaced by a way that means you will eventually exhaust your retirement account. If you can create inexhaustible income streams, paying for necessities becomes a little less difficult and the enjoyment of your day more enjoyable since you will know that you can survive without a job, business, or practice. You decide to work. Replacing possessions is a difficult thing to explain. If you have young children, you no doubt spend weekends earning money and then spend your days off buying new furniture, appliances, and clothing that your children, pets, and husband have destroyed. You certainly could not afford to take long vacations or buy expensive cars and expensive goods. Since the vast majority of Americans cannot live indefinitely without an income, the political obligations are enormous. Take another look at B.13.

Diversifying Income Streams

Every type of income has its own characteristic: working as an employee, you have a job, thereby earning an employment income; if you work full-time for yourself, you have your own business, a small business income; if you don't have time to earn regular income, you don't need it, but you do have assets, the rent is your asset income; the annual dividends received in part are a distribution of income from shareholders or partners, but you cannot rely on the dividends as the main source of income to live on; the company has profit, it gives you salary and benefits, the income like Employment income; and the government pays you allowances, pensions and child support, the income sources at the opposite end of the Social Security scale. Each of these income characteristics, in different ways, reflects the economic status of wage earners and different economy, and the relationship of tax status to income. Lacking the basic life education of the economy makes many people bypass the hedge of financial management. If they are suddenly fired and cannot find a job in the economic depression, unemployment payment is only 60% of the previous employment income, so the dependence of work for life is the 'new' reality. The loss of the 'work' life income brings a desperate living pressure to crush people's confidence and dignity. They lost faith and dignity completely and were reluctant to accept material and emotional assistance. Besides, the sources of income, work and other labels attach to us, creating mediocrity, lack of dignity, and reluctance to experience the common existence of various income that causes underground financial pressures. The economic foundation of society makes us uneasy about discussing them and taboo. On the other hand, many people have entered the silent anxiety of not getting rid of poverty. Since modern education and social system mainly takes economic types as an example to shape people's psychological state, what should we do to reduce our income, decrease our income risk, and increase our wealth? The answer is to diversify our sources of income. This chapter discusses each income characteristic in addition to providing a general introduction. It can help the reader to understand the relationship between remuneration and the economy, and also understand that wages are different from other types of income due to their special economic status. Based on income characteristics, this chapter also provides a series of practical strategies to help readers reduce income risks, decrease income vulnerability, and increase the possibilities for own welfare.

Diversification is a financial concept that most people are familiar with. Essentially, it means 'don't put all your eggs in one basket' - spread the risk. If you invest all your money in one type of asset (property, for example), all your assets are equally beholden to the variables that can affect property - and that goes for income too. So if something happens in the economy that affects the property market, you are dangerously overexposed. Diversification is one of the keys to financial freedom, but normally it is only talked about in terms of investment. You are encouraged to diversify to reduce the risk of financial loss. But this book is not about how to sort out your finances - most people have no assets or wealth to speak of - it's about ensuring that you have a broad base of sources from which to receive your income. In essence, diversification diversifies your lifestyle economy, not your lifestyle.

Building Passive Income

So, in our area of wealth building, the important goal is to establish many sources of ongoing income that can produce substantial monthly money from a modest sum. Successful examples of passive income include the money earned in the floats or reserves of an insurance company and the income earned from the investments within IRAs and 401(k) Plans, just to name a few. The easiest way for most people to establish multiple sources of passive income over time is to accumulate as many assets as possible which, in turn, provide the positive cash flow that results from the income that they generate.

One of the most important strategies for achieving financial freedom as quickly as possible is to establish multiple sources of passive income. It is difficult to accumulate substantial wealth by earning only active income. Most successful people have learned that putting your money to work for you can be the fastest way to collect more of the green stuff. The concept is actually quite simple. Generally speaking, passive income is that income you earn by working to establish the arrangement to produce the income, and after that, earning the income while you are not working or working only a little. Some forms of passive income are tax-free; others are taxed at much lower rates than active income!

CHAPTER 7

Real Estate Investments

Hold steady. If you know what you want to achieve, you will. The most important quality to have is determination. All real estate investments can fail. It is possible that investments in real estate are less likely to fail than other investment forms. The more quickly you want to achieve your financial freedom, the more you will want to consider using these strategies for property investment.

Many people around the world have earned substantial wealth by investing in real estate. All these people have had one thing in common: they have been persistent in their property investment. Property investment is nothing to be scared of. With a bit of hard work and determination, one can achieve massive success in property investment. Property management is a large part of investment. Property investment can be easy if you have nothing else to do, or if you do have another job, you can rely on a property management company.

Benefits of Real Estate Investments

Another feature that distinguishes real estate capital from financial capital is that it can be used as a physical prospect in various ways, provided that the real estate is used and managed correctly by professionals. Despite the maintenance costs that need to be incurred to prevent devaluation and the risk associated with poor liquidity, real estate should be considered as an asset which can promote optimal security of capital invested and a substantial rise in long-term value.

One of the significant differences between real estate investments and investments in other types of assets lies in the fact that, through proper management procedures and techniques, it is possible to obtain benefits from real estate without using up its physical mass. Unlike industrial investments, where capital is at risk on a daily basis, the investor in a real estate investment is not exposed to this risk.

Real estate investment is a form of capital accumulation which stands out for its unique characteristics, as well as being a type of investment favored by private investors for practical, historical, and psychological reasons.

Strategies for Investing in Real Estate

Real estate offers the opportunity to earn ongoing cash returns and passive appreciation, while at the same time providing favorable tax treatment. Real estate also serves as a good hedge against inflation. Let's look at three strategies for investing in real estate. Information on tax advantages and disadvantages of each strategy is provided in the appendix.

1. Buying and holding real estate. A classic real estate investment strategy is to buy single-family homes, multi-family properties, or commercial properties and then rent them out to long-term tenants. The benefits include earning rental income, getting tax advantages, and experiencing appreciation as the property increases in value. The challenges are that real estate can require a substantial amount of money from the owner, tenants can choose not to pay, and an unexpected expense, such as a roof or a furnace repair, can eat into a year's worth of income.

2. Flipping real estate. Real estate flipping—also known as rehabbing—has been glorified by television shows such as Flip This House. The drawbacks are that buyers pay a steep price for flipping a house into good condition, and the time and stress required to oversee the renovations can easily turn a potential profit into a disaster.

3. Real estate investment trusts (REITs). REITs allow investors to participate in the income-producing profits from real estate without having to purchase the properties themselves. They are a solid investment for diversifying a portfolio and are a fairly liquid investment. The major disadvantage of REITs is that while they provide a stream of current income, the shares do not hold appreciatory value.

CHAPTER 8

Entrepreneurship and Business Ownership

Versatility: A small business has innumerable facets. Owners must possess the versatility to wear many hats. Frequently, they are both chief executive officer and chief financial officer. And chief marketing officer. And chief operating officer. The list goes on and on...

Excellence: A propensity for quality and achievement separates successful entrepreneurs from the less successful. Entrepreneurs are typically the kind of people who view disappointment and rejection as challenges that can be overcome. They tend to be very competitive and desire power over their own destinies.

Self-assurance: A resilient personality is indispensable because very few startups become great successes. Upon becoming entrepreneurs, many former employees find that they are not sufficiently perseverant in the face of adversity.

Whereas building wealth through stocks or real estate is the product of sound money management and the employment of certain techniques, entrepreneurship—starting, operating, and succeeding in a business—is subject to the condition that one has the proper psychological disposition, personal attributes, and aptitude for capitalism. Not everyone is cut out to be an entrepreneur. Although there are exceptions, the following seven characteristics have been found to be deterministic:

Starting a Business

The old ABC Salesman Motto: Always, Be, Closing holds true today for networking as well. Always form and nurture connections. You never know what, when, or where your next connection or source will come from. I feel cold calling and hiring decisions go together. It's even more important to have a gut feeling when you are not face to face with your potential business connection. You need to be able to tell if you are compatible by phone and get professional help to aid this process if needed. Small companies grow into big companies because they attract good people and keep them. The network aspect mentioned in every area of management is crucial to how we perceive the company and judge as an overall entity.

80 percent of all new business is began by people over the age of 35. This leaves some 20 percent who haven't reached their 35th year the advantage of experience from older entrepreneurs. In my view, it's not the business idea, it's about networking, wherever you go and whatever you do. This includes always treating everyone you come into contact with, whether goal related or not, with respect. I believe that all new companies succeed or fail based on the quality of both people they are able to attract and keep. Management ability is your most important asset. This quality can be seen before hiring, spending time in person or with a sample of work, ideally detailed extensive background checks. Embellishment will not give you positive feedback, it will cause a waste of time and money on an employee or employees that are not right for the job. There will be differences of opinions in any organization. With prior knowledge, you will not miss crucial hiring situations.

You've probably heard some of the how-to lists for success but do you know what the qualities of a successful entrepreneur really are? Before you start your business, you might want to take a look at some of the more compelling habits and traits of successful entrepreneurs and adopt them for your own.

Small business tax breaks come under the heading of deductions from gross income on the front of form 1040. Business investment and motivation to work for yourself as tax deductions can really reduce the net cost of being your own boss. If you currently have a job where Social Security and other employee benefits are paid, due to employment taxes you've probably noticed that they absorb about one-quarter of your income quite automatically. Then to add a nearly 10% tax bite on your earnings from employment to provide revenue to the government's coffers, while you are struggling to build both your security and independence, is more than a little bit disheartening. There's always some tax on income from any source but when you are both employer and employee you get an opportunity to take advantage of the tax laws that were custom written to reward small business.

Big profits come from big risks, but proven small business tax breaks make that plunge a bit less fearful. These breaks are the same kind big business has used for years. Here's how to determine the tax benefits to help you make your decision to start your business.

Scaling and Growth Strategies

The restaurant and car repair owner may never have the growth opportunity as the investor in a publicly-traded company. The business models of both start out with one location and grow additional locations every year to take advantage of the proven sales at each company location. It is likely that real estate investors and the Small Business Administration may finance the additions. Businesses that only make money by having one retail business at a time may choose to reinvest its profits in a business that may stay on the fast-growth trajectory. A successful restaurant and car repair business model designed to grow could be worth ten years of cap. If the company can make even more sales and earnings by having regional, national, and international locations, then the competitor cap rates for the industry are around twenty times the annual sales.

Once you have a profitable business model that is repeatable and scalable, it is time to offer your investors the opportunity for scale and growth. You may start by inviting family members and friends to invest in your company. If your business is a restaurant or a car repair business, you are unlikely to see any appreciation in your company except through your control over earnings. That may only be worth about two to four years of your annual sales if you wish to sell. However, if you could grow the business to $10M in sales in three years and maintain that growth, you can sell the business five years later for about ten times that $10M in annual sales. That would compete favorably with the annual sales of a publicly-traded company in that industry. All a cap rate does is relate the total market value for the public company with the annual sales, which can be called cap or capitalization sales. It is the same formula as relating earnings to sales. Businesses in other industries are evaluated similarly in earnings and sales.

CHAPTER 9

Retirement Planning

There are numerous financial planning software programs available that make the retirement planning process relatively straightforward. They can present varying scenarios and can be used to reflect differing combinations of future years of labor income, retirement asset bases and contribution levels, investment returns, and life expectancies. By inputting a variety of parameters, you can measure the potential impact on your financial freedom and the viability of wealth-building strategies that you might consider, including spending reductions, investment risk reduction, and asset allocation shifts.

While saving and investing for retirement are important guideposts in the quest for financial freedom, they are just that—guideposts to the bigger picture of living life your way. By envisioning what you want your life to be like at age 65 and capturing it in the context of setting up a long-term financial plan, you can move toward the goal of creating your imminent reality in the most straightforward manner. The amount of money you need to save in order to accumulate enough resources to successfully support your life at age 65 largely depends on the asset base that you accumulate, the rate of return that your investments generate, the amount of money that you save and invest, and the number of years remaining until you reach the blessed day when you can chuck it all in.

Importance of Retirement Planning

Today's greater life expectancy has radically changed the concept of retirement. You could spend 20 or 30 years in retirement. Your retirement years could be the most gratifying time of your life, a time when you're free to follow your interests. Provided that you're financially prepared, these years can be full of opportunities. However, without proper preparation, they could also be a time of frustration and disappointment. Would you rather spend those golden years planning for the future or trying to make ends meet? The choice is yours. Start funding your retirement account now. And remember, the contributions of money and time you invest now can have a significant effect on your lifestyle in retirement.

The importance of retirement planning shouldn't be underestimated. Without adequate retirement savings, you could spend your final years struggling to make ends meet. It's daunting to consider the possibility of going from a comfortable, full-time job to living on a fixed income, but simple changes now could go a long way toward securing your future. By establishing your retirement goals, setting a budget that accounts for savings, and investing in both employer-sponsored accounts and individual accounts, you'll have the proper tools to enjoy financial freedom when you're through working.

Options for Retirement Accounts

What investment options are available for retirement accounts, and what investment choices should be made in those accounts?

Options for Retirement Accounts A variety of investment options can be used in retirement accounts. Many plans offer a choice of a number of actively managed mutual funds. Other investment options can include common stock, bonds, and various types of money market securities. A growing number of retirement plans offer index funds as an investment choice. The investment in an index fund involves lower average expenses than do actively managed funds, since the portfolio in the index accounts is an average of the portfolio of all the funds.

The specific investment opportunities offered to participants in a retirement plan are described in the plan's Disclosure Statement. This statement provides detailed information about the investment options, including objectives, risks, and expenses. If the investment option is a mutual fund, the plan participant can also use standard mutual fund reports to evaluate the fund's investment performance. Every actively managed mutual fund registered with the Securities and Exchange Commission (SEC) is required to disclose, at least annually in a prospectus, its investment performance for the last five years. The mutual fund reports, which provide for more timely, concise information, can be accessed via the internet. The prospective investor may find this information by visiting the website of the fund family or by visiting one of a few web-based mutual fund services.

CHAPTER 10

Estate Planning and Wealth Transfer

We highly recommend continuing to hold a comprehensive financial planning session with advisors to review the accounting, legal, asset protection, taxation, inheritance and family strategic implications of the investment advisory strategies and objectives. Always seek advanced counsel in estate planning and wealth transfer matters as they are continually changing with the evolution of family values, employment, retirement, healthcare and privacy. Success often profits entirely from each individual's ability to preserve and protect a portion of their life - that creates financial wealth sufficient for wealth transfers.

Estate planning is the final aspect of financial freedom. Nearly everyone has an interest in the priorities and structure of their estate. However, the importance of this process has been dwarfed by the innovation of reducing estate and inheritance taxes while at the same time creating meaningful income and wealth for family members and friends. We highly value the opinions and insight of the estate planning specialists that have shared their firsthand experiences and have contributed meaningful insight. There are few more supportive of making meaningful and lasting estate plans that can protect a lifetime of hard work, discipline and financial acumen.

Creating an Estate Plan

It is important for the reader to recognize that estate planning can be more than just protecting the fruit of one's labor after death. It can also incorporate strategies for taking care of the people you care about in life. A full set of tools and advice for estate planning is beyond our expertise, but some common sense can help. Specifically, even before the demise of your physical being, you need to consider making provisions for periods of potential incapacity. The appointment of a medical proxy to make healthcare decisions is necessary, as is a financial proxy to conduct financial transactions. A simple will can specify how to handle the passage of assets from one generation to the next. Finally, the reader should examine the need for insurance coverage related to estate planning, including liquidity to cover the potential need to pay taxes associated with the estate.

Estate planning is literally where the rubber meets the road on the issue of control. Unless you take it seriously, a lot of hard work shaping your life's activities could ultimately be wasted because your spouse, partner, family, friends, or charity might end up with less than you expected. To the extent that one's death can ever be dealt with in any joyous fashion, estate planning is something you do for yourself and for those you leave behind. The government dictates an estate plan for you that many people do not take the time to examine. Although government-mandated guidelines might not do real damage, your desires are unlikely to be met unless you express them in a legally binding fashion before it is too late. The proper legal documents include a will, a living will, medical powers of attorney, financial powers of attorney, and perhaps a trust to avoid probate.

Minimizing Estate Taxes

In sum, this part of the book will point out that very substantial reductions in terminal-tax costs are possible and that the savings will persist on a cumulative lifetime basis for those who carefully plan for the inevitable transfer. The key to such planning is the making and implementing of timely year-end family decisions. Either direct gift giving or setting up a brand new open-end tax-wise family trust. Gain control of the new trust now! Furthermore, note also that this book will devote far more space to the subject of the control feature of the Adam Smith Capitalist Trust and, in fact, will devote the first section to its complete analysis. Since the Trust upsets the conventional present-day estate planning, it will afford tax-wasted Americans substantial freedom from what otherwise would be their pitfalls to financial salvation. With God visible in the bottom line, trust no two lawyers to program their new federal mega-tax implant device in anything but the most benevolent (for them!) fashion possible. It ensures success in generating their professional fees in Conservative Valhalla.

As we have already indicated, the general cut in income taxes achieved in the U.S. in 1981 included a significant reduction in the previously imposed penalties for dying. In other words, the estate tax, the gift tax, and the generation-skipping tax - all three - were drastically reduced, and there are strong indications that a further reduction in the estate tax burden likely will occur in the years to come. Consequently, this book could easily have avoided the subject of estate tax minimization. We have not done so for a number of very good reasons: First, because of the ever-changing nature of tax legislation, may advice to make direct gifts (or tax-wise trusts) possible - five or ten years prior to envisaged death - to those junior family members who will be the ultimate inheritors of personal wealth and thus gain the maximum advantages of long-term tax-exempt appreciation.

CHAPTER 11

Financial Education and Literacy

The second point is that financial education, or financial literacy, must be given as a discipline in the curriculums of all levels and in short courses. I also teach commercial courses and one thing I've seen in a few teachers is that they make the students practically ready to become capitalists. This happens with many institutions of education. The schools and colleges are failing the students, who do not receive commerce education. Besides, they grow up being employees of others and not employers. The business programs in schools are great for the employee interested in improving the quality of his business. I do not want to do it, but I can pass it on to someone to transform into a business is another one I can do it now, so why not do it? Build your destiny!

The problem of financial education and literacy is an area that needs urgent action. The first step for achieving wealth and financial freedom is education. This means we must all be committed to gaining knowledge and learning about the science of finance. Universities have been part of the problem because we believe that education is the way to get out of a financial nightmare. As an instructor, we have a saying that goes like this: "If you're unable to create wealth for yourself, how are you going to do it for the company?" Universities also indulge in fantasies because most of the ideas are subjective, based on what is written in the books. For me, being a teacher made me gain this understanding in my class. Maybe you're asking now, "Why are you still there if you feel this way?" The answer is that I believe that everything can change if some professors open their minds to commerce and entrepreneurial experiences.

Importance of Financial Education

Financial education is so important because the rules explaining how money works are not like the general tenets of other subjects such as calculus, biology, or history. If one jumps off a bridge, one will fall: this is an immutable rule. However, several immutable rules exist in the world of money yet every day, we see people with impeccable educations who manage to ignore them. No one has ever returned home with a degree in calculus, having failed to learn any of the tenets. Math follows a series of rules: one can finish school without understanding how they work, but in order to solve problems, one must have an understanding of them. If one completes a course in neuroscience, one will have a professional understanding of how the human brain functions. If one leaves school without the ability to recount the ways that money can escape from their wallet, how to invest wisely, or which entities hold the power to influence economic matters, they failed a key class in preparing for financial freedom.

It is strange that after years of sitting through lectures from kindergarten through high school and then through whatever number of long years spent at institutes of higher learning, people emerge with little understanding of the subject of money. If the subject of money is taught at all in school, it is economics, and economics does not teach people about money. A student can spend years in economics classes from grade school right on through university without ever hearing the word money or knowing very much at all about how money works. A student learns nothing about the rules regarding money or about the different areas of money, such as spending, saving, investing, and the importance of understanding the role that the creation of money plays in their life.

Resources for Learning

That said, you must still find a good place to start. Joining a finance course is probably the first and best response. By taking notes, doing homework, and finishing readings, you can get up to speed much quicker than you could learning on your own because you can get instant feedback from the professor or teaching assistants. You also will interact with other students who will ask questions and bring up points which never occurred to you, good or bad. This aspect might be the most important. If you are the only person asking questions about the models you have learned, you will get no improvement in the learning process. Stimulating conversation that covers the motivations behind the models and the implementation or use of the models is indispensable. That is why we always put a strong emphasis on FAQs, Frequently Asked Questions, and their answers, in our CAMEL Database.

Suppose you are in the mood to learn about stock valuation models or portfolio management or anything else. Where do you start? In the entire realm of financial literature, you could spend your entire life getting nowhere, for it seems that no matter how many conclusions these models seem to reach, an equal amount of questions always seems to be left unanswered. Although it sounds like nothing but problems, we love the puzzle aspect of this study; that is why we are involved in the research aspect of the endeavor.

CHAPTER 12

Mindset and Psychology of Wealth

Rich people believe "I create my life." Poor people believe "Life happens to me". Successful people take responsibility for the part they play, clear up their limiting beliefs and negative conditioning, and move their mental obstacles out of the way. Personal responsibility is the philosophical foundation for wealth building because in the end only you can decide what you deserve and earn. Success comes from your own thoughts and actions. It's always a personal choice; no one else in the world will determine it for you. Find wealth-building models that work, seek to understand those models and then develop habits that make you effective in executing those models in the world in which we operate today. Wholeness can be a harmonious blending of health, family, career, spirituality. When you are whole and balanced your financial life also falls into place.

"It's about the money, and it's not." When it comes to building wealth and financial independence, the mental aspects are at least as important as the financial strategies you choose. If you don't believe you can be financially free—or if you have hidden fears about becoming independent—you'll experience paralysis during your wealth-building journey. Rich people are courageous. Poor people are frightened. If you believe in yourself and in your financial dreams, if you're willing to take calculated risks, and if you're brave enough to stare down your fears... you position yourself to win. It's as simple—and as difficult—as that. Knowledge is important. Money like the understanding of wealth-building and money-making principles. But money experts usually stress that success is 80% psychology and 20% mechanics. With a money blueprint embedded in the subconscious mind, the 20% of mechanics will automatically follow.

Developing a Wealth Mindset

Just as important as money in determining high achievement is confidence in one's abilities. Even abilities that are not as perfect as they might be will be of little help if not accompanied by the self-assurance that inspires those abilities. When we look back, we can see that every new development and discovery we have ever made becomes a piece of actuality. Every individual has been created with an inherently perceptive, directive, judicial, innovative, strategic, and impressionated nature. For the development of these unique features, it is important to understand that a genius was not considered so because of his education, learning, or wisdom on all subjects known to man. Instead, it was the power and application of his creativity, which he brought to one specific subject and the discipline with which he achieved established success. Nothing worthwhile arises from anything but diversified creativity and an unceasing desire to be better than willing to seek and shape the knowledge that leads to self-mastery. The history of civilization is a story of human interests engaged in the task of progress. It is driven by the relentless creative urge of human interest invoking creativity as change and renewal becomes a refining process in the knowledge and search for satisfaction. The study of individual human motivational variations is important in attempts to interpret consumer behavior. This role suggests that purchasing decisions are heavily influenced by a group of stimulating, compelling, and triggering factors, or motives. Once these motives are activated, the individual is not only energized but aware of the urge that fuels action to achieve monetary and spiritual satisfaction. Market success depends on the ability to understand clearly the desires of the market, as seen in the products or services that capture the needs and desires of these desires. The stimulants that ignite the desire to buy become motivational desires. They vary in strength, depending on flashes of pleasant or unpleasant feelings involving monetary and spiritual goals. When effectively nurtured, these motives become motive-activating mechanisms that regulate the pursuit of satisfaction and fulfillment.

There are two "wings" needed for financial flight: one born of inspiration, creativity, vision, and motivation, and the other rooted in formal knowledge, research, and analysis. Visualization takes off when the statistics of the chance to win are known. Both wings must be employed to launch into orbit, taking into account that only a few carry the urge to have wings. Napoleon Hill lists some of the distinguishing features found in outstanding individuals: the successful individual has learned to do something everyone else cannot do in an outstanding way. To perform at a higher level, one must have definite plans and goals best suited for the talents, abilities, and aptitudes available. The drive and thrust for achievement lie in the multitude of plans that back up dreams, goals, and ideas, and the strategic combinations can be limitless. These motivate us to forge ahead, acquire new knowledge, widen experiences, test many possibilities, and strive to do that which we love.

Overcoming Limiting Beliefs

As money attracts money, it is a wonderful cosmic law when understood correctly and used in a very positive way. You must be strong-willed and determined to get to be what you want financially to achieve. So many people are just waiting for the big money to come to them. It is very important to understand that you must go to the money. It is not coming to you. The money is patiently waiting for you to find it. Magnetic wealth, the more you give, the more you get. The more you receive, the more you will be able to give. In turn, the universe will then respond accordingly to your other financial needs and wants, because you have learned the secret of the importance of keeping money in circulation. There should be a constant flow in and then out. You cannot afford to loan money and control money; you are not the master over money. The more money you have, the more you are in a position to give.

Start paying attention to your day-to-day money conversations or your most recent internal money dialogues. What beliefs were expressed? Study all your past financial decisions; all your beliefs led to these relationship choices. Most people hold negative beliefs about money deep in their subconscious mind that sabotage their every attempt of breaking through the invisible ceiling that is controlling their lives, preventing them from reaching the life and business they would really like to have. All day long, you are scrutinizing and appraising yourself inspired by all your limiting beliefs about money, which are determining your failure or success, as to what your personal experience is going to deliver.

Until you change your beliefs about money and about wealth, your income will experience an invisible ceiling. If your self-image and beliefs about your abilities are set at the earning ability of \$50,000, \$30,000, or \$250,000, that is pretty much what you will attract. Your outer world can never outperform your inner world. It is not your outer world that is the problem; it is your inner world that needs changing. You will only earn what you subconsciously decide you are allowed to earn. Because your environment always reflects what you have proved to yourself consciously or subconsciously. And you must become rich in your mind first, before you become rich in your life, because only when you get successful on the inside will you have the power to manifest it on the outside. The reason more people are not rich today is because they have the same belief system they had yesterday and prior years, and therefore they are unable to deliver the world what it wants and needs.

CHAPTER 13

Long-Term Financial Planning

Even without inflation, the future use of accumulated financial resources, money saved or profits reinvested, will provide a prime resource control planning problem. The proper use of this money requires careful, detailed plans to be made months and/or years ahead. The overall role of long-term financial planning will be presented next followed by a detailed presentation of the time pattern of the planning future. The results of proper long-term planning also measure financial indicators of business success. They provide working papers for long-range formal and financial agreements such as contracts between organizations and for the court-ordered divorce. Proper application of family work-time resources also help to resolve some of the family's income distribution planning problems.

The control of financial resources requires a plan for the use of these funds. Proper long-range planning can solve most business/personal financial resource use problems by anticipating and identifying change now. In a noninflationary world, long-range planning would not be as important since business firm sales revenues, costs, and expenses would be limited to means and longer-term horizons.

Since financial resources are affected by inflation, the planning problem becomes more severe. Prices that have doubled in one year, for instance, require a business firm to plan for excessive sales to provide enough resources just to keep even when business real revenues are considered.

Setting Financial Goals

An understanding of your ability to absorb risk, and your other priorities, will help to ensure that you make the appropriate investment choices. You can adjust the growth potential, risk, and tax consequences of your investment strategy to more closely match your other characteristics.

Each of these goals has a different risk, timeframe, and volatility (danger). You can do very well with a short-term goal using a simple savings account, while you will want to look at something with a bit more risk and potential reward for long-term goals. A retirement portfolio may use several different investment types, including equities (stocks), bonds, cash, and special retirement accounts and special guaranteed insurance accounts to meet various goals and objectives.

- Short Term - Emergency fund, savings for major upcoming purchases, like a vacation or holiday spending. - Medium Term - Funds for major purchases, like a car or home, period of unemployment. - Long Term - Pay for higher education, retirement.

You should always have a clear understanding of what you are trying to achieve. The financial system is a scary place to wander without a destination in mind. It's like driving a car without a clear destination, will you eventually run out of gas? Financial goals generally fit into the following goals:

Creating a Long-Term Plan

If you know where you're going, any road will get you there. If you don't know where you're going, all the roads in the world won't get you there.

Make a detailed map of your most important goals and dreams. What will you need to do first to help you get from where you are to where you want to go? What order and time frame do those intermediate goals and dreams need to be set or completed in? Whether you have 20 years or 5 years to achieve your dreams, the journey can be overwhelming if you don't know how to divide it into workable bites. Concentrate on achieving your goals one step at a time and take a good look at the personal and the financial potential that you already have. Next, carefully select one or two new areas that you would like to develop. Start with those you can realistically achieve in the short term. As you succeed, and you will, make sure to celebrate. Then go ahead and create new opportunities for further growth.

There are not many people who (right now) have all the skills which are necessary to achieve all they want on their own. Happily, this situation usually does not last. Keep growing and keep developing yourself, specifically in the areas which are related to your friends, your personal growth, and your career. With time and effort, the experience will increase too. With this experience, you will develop a greater power to achieve your goals and dreams.

CHAPTER 14

Monitoring and Adjusting Financial Strategies

Adjusting financial strategies is an ongoing process throughout a person's life. It is necessary because goals and personal circumstances change over time as people age, and evolve through educational attainment, personal relationships, and career stages. Performance of financial products and services selected for investing and other purposes will also influence whether planned amounts of income are generated and required amounts of money are maintained. Influence on personal satisfaction and the community's economy can result from changes in personal circumstances, needs, and goals, and market conditions, tax laws, and other major factors. Practical tactics for monitoring and fine-tuning financial plans are also presented. They apply to all stages of the life cycle for income, consumption, investing, and income protection activities.

Monitoring progress is essential in financial planning. It will tell how well financial strategies are working and allow timely corrections. It will also reflect changes in personal circumstances, needs, and goals, market conditions, tax laws, and other factors. Monitoring can be done at three levels—relying on personal review, engaging professional review, or using personal finance software and simple spreadsheet programs. Factors to monitor include savings and investment plan performance, home ownership objectives, insurance and principal protection needs, tax liability, and the economy's impact. Prudent dedication, time, and discipline are needed to ensure the best financial results over time.

Tracking Progress

Reviewing what you've done is an integral part of the entire planning process; because what you are doing today is not just related to the future, but it is the present state of your plan. There may be some actions taken now that could change the trajectory of what happens in the future, or could give more options to react to different situations. For example, a change in monthly savings amount that helps you reach that key position of lower debts, and you can begin to explore new opportunities rather than face no options but to work until your dying day. A change in monthly saving amount could also put you in a position to allow you to live life more in accord with your values, and therefore, enjoy a richer, fulfilling life.

We have already touched on the importance of taking an accounting of all areas of our financial plan. Look at each and every year, no matter how unimportant each figure may seem, in the outcome of a great financial plan. Over a time of five or ten years, small amounts can accumulate and double and then double again. At the end of the five or ten years, you have over a few thousand dollars.

You should be able to track your progress after you have carefully defined what financial freedom means to you. Develop your plan and begin to track how you are doing for each of the areas. Be patient and realize that progress usually will come in a step fashion. Not overnight will everything fall in place according to your life goals. Nonetheless, you should always be moving toward financial freedom; always try to do something - no matter how small - to further your dreams. Don't let what is happening today keep you from your goals or from finishing your plan.

Making Adjustments as Needed

The general point is that being serious about getting control over your own financial future is not simply a brief exercise. The related activities, mostly but not exclusively action items, will continue in one form or another, day in and day out, for the rest of your life. While the three strategies may be atypical for you at first, following them is very much about what you do every day in terms of social and professional activities, or investing your resources of time, energy, and money. Patterns not only of spending or investing, but also of self-organizing, decision-making, and self-education are usually involved. Examples include job, career, and educational choices, developing specific initiative to start or expand financial activities, the speed and forms of entrepreneurial activities, selecting specific financial intermediaries, and developing individual savings and investment plans. Be prepared. After achieving financial independence, your financial life will be different in many respects. The changes give new and brighter opportunities to live interesting, fulfilling, satisfying, and possibly extraordinary lives. Changes, if introduced systematically and patiently today, will prepare you for the transformation. Many of these, but not all, can be revised as needed in the future.

No matter what form it takes, once you have designed your DIY plan, it is not cast in stone. As with any plan, if its execution proves less than perfect or the environment it operates in undergoes change, the plan may need to be modified, postponed, or even scrapped. This is also true of the three strategies. Designing a plan to free oneself from financial dependence is a complicated process, and problems will inevitably arise. The moment they materialize and are discovered, such problems need to be addressed systematically and replaced with better ways of executing the plan. This booklet covers a few of the most common problems and possible solutions.

CHAPTER 15

Building a Support Network

Furthermore, few are likely to support you or understand why you wish to do things differently to them. Be warned if you attempt new things, by definition, you are doing something new and untried. This is the best and quickest way to have everyone trying to talk you out of your direction. This is the way that it is with humans. The vast majority are followers and your new direction indirectly challenges them and their beliefs by extension. In seeking a support group for your wealth-building goals, you should try to surround yourself with individuals who are similar to you in both mind and actions. Those who can help you to build the wealth and the life you aspire to.

There is a popular adage that all wealthy people know each other. This highlights the fact that wealthy and successful people tend to flock together and are comfortable in each other's company. Becoming rich and successful on your own can be a lonely and daunting experience. It is certainly easier when you have the moral encouragement and practical advice of others to help you on your journey. If you are self-employed or are running your own business, or are doing anything out of the ordinary or a little left of center, you will find that the vast majority of people in your life will not understand what you are doing or the direction you are heading.

Importance of a Support System

I also value that every parent should keep in mind that your kids aren't going to be all kids in your lifetime. There will come a time when they will start living their lives their way. All they have gotten from you will be their memories and the habits that you'll have instilled in them. Hopefully, they lead happy lives through basics that you'll have got from you. Teach them the "Do Self" concept by developing a doing self habit in them. It's not necessarily the amount of time we spend with our kids that is, it's all about the quality of that time. Oh, I forget to mention. Don't you think it's strange that we refer to spending time with our kids as "quality time"? Does the phrase "quantity time" seem more appropriate? Just a thought.

Once you've talked things over with your potential partner and with yourself, it's helpful to spend a little more time thinking about the role you want "Doing Family" to play in your life. The next three articles will be a series, focusing on the concept of 'Family' in the broader context. The key phrase in the following exchange is 'quality time'. To save this and any heated discussions in small groups that might arise from the idea of 'quality time', lean the resolution being placed forth by Ezekiel.

Networking and Mentorship

I have always found it interesting that those who succeed seem to have the same story. Metaphorically, they met someone who said someone knew someone who could help. Networkers seem to know everyone and have an outgoing personality. They seem to value friendships and genuinely care about others' well-being. In return for their kind dispositions and helpful natures, opportunity comes knocking at their door. A similar principle is responsible for a high-school reunion phenomenon: many times the people who attend reunions and through voluntary committees become involved in the planning of these events are those who are motivated to help each other. As a result, those individuals become privy to new business opportunities and other information that has the potential to lead to relevant new professional and personal relationships.

It's often been said that whom you know can be as important as what you know. This is particularly pertinent in the world of entrepreneurial effort. Asking people questions and drawing upon each other's strengths is one of the greatest strengths of free enterprise. Discussions with other like-minded people can put problems into perspective and short-circuit a negative mindset before it takes hold of you. Hobbies that bring you in contact with other entrepreneurs and business-minded individuals can be perfect venues. The more often you work to improve your networking and sales skills, the more effective you become. If you are uncomfortable when speaking with authority, the best way to conquer that fear is to become involved in many situations where authority is necessary.

CHAPTER 16

Financial Freedom for Different Life Stages

Despite dislocations in personal or public sector plans or strategies, people need to develop short- and long-term financial plans to live their lives more freely and confidently, perhaps more comfortably, and even potentially more securely later in life. In practical terms, for instance, married people should plan for a secure old age together, though individually, as well as separately. This chapter suggests some useful financial strategies for the earlier years and middle years of people's productive work lives, as well as financial strategies for the stage in people's lives when they are more likely to no longer work full time. As aging and health improvements continue to redistribute life expectancies worldwide, there is a growing need to put financial considerations in a more comprehensive context that includes family, career, health, involvement in society, environment, and changes in public and private sector policies, in the search of life quality and meaning.

Many principles of sound financial management are ageless, as are strategies for building wealth and bringing it to bear to achieve financial freedom. Nevertheless, the types of challenges people face often change as they mature and their careers, financial resources, and family and other responsibilities evolve. Different temporal stages of life affect what people can realistically hope to accomplish and perhaps even what they should strive for when managing their financial affairs. The changes people experience in terms of family or career choices, health, the environment, other aspects of society, or public and private sector policies necessitate adjustments in the financial strategies they select and the tactics they use to carry out those strategies.

Financial Planning for Young Adults

Amarillo College in Amarillo, Texas, recognizes the importance of early financial planning. In the budget and money management class, personal and occupational education is the goal. "Even if they are in debt, it's better that they know how to get out of it," says instructor Gayle Binion. Although economic and personal situations can vary among this group, young people are developing core financial planning skills. They're using available technology or seeking one-on-one counseling to help them and have grasped the basics of establishing financial independence. Most importantly, they seem to have a more long-term view of achieving financial goals. Therefore, the basics are not overlooked. They include simple planning strategies that encourage students to delay gratification and live a prudent, cautious lifestyle. They force them to ask themselves such questions as "What if my major were constructional deferred through the use of public funds? In addition to limiting investment opportunities, would I limit my ability to work comfortably today? Is satisfying my desire for instant gratification more important than my future?"

Part of being an adult is understanding the many financial decisions that lay ahead. As young adults, the necessity of exercising sound financial judgment can sometimes be difficult to see. And yet not all of today's youth are ill-prepared to face the future. In fact, many are ready to take on what lies ahead. Today's youth are aware of the need to delay instant gratification and are making choices that reflect their long-term financial goals. These people aren't living for today, they're living for tomorrow and are going to do well. They are saving, creating wealth, and are more than likely on their way to a comfortable retirement.

Financial Strategies for Mid-Career Professionals

Mid-Career Strategies for Financial Freedom

There are several objectives financial planning advisors will commonly suggest for someone in the thick of his or her profession, say from age 40 to 55. First and foremost, to paraphrase the classic saying of the spending of money, the beginning of wisdom is to save. Ensuring the financial independence of your retirement years is an imperative. Next, properly insuring yourself, both to increase your estate and protect it from catastrophic loss, should be an immediate objective. Finally, to the extent your estate is considered to be of significant value, a concerted effort should be made to provide for the future competence of your children or grandchildren. A generous education allowance is always beneficial.

Ripe Research and Resources

If you are hitting your high earning years, around or about 40, and your investment portfolio is not where it should be, remember hope. In the same hands and the same time frame, hope has a great track record! The can't-lose-20 percent-of-everything-you-earn game has made more people wealthy than has hiring brilliant money managers. Money managers don't work for free, and often the ones that offer the best return can't be paid to handle small accounts. That's great for them, not so good for you. Be honest with yourself. If you are 40 and don't have enough assets to retire in 30 or 40 years, you need to take some assignments that will quickly raise your net financial worth.

CHAPTER 17

Financial Freedom in Retirement

Some people never retire, but more people want a different life in retirement than they have while working full-time. This desire is not so much a question of having the money to do it, as it is about what do you want to do with your time. Having an income is a necessary part of being able to live with the independence that provides the wealth-building exercise. When you retire from a job, or a career, no matter in what retirement plan you are involved, you are essentially stopping the stream of money coming into your collective retirement saving accounts, and allowing these accounts now to act as a form of income for your needs. It is really that simple and that complex. Compound interest is double the fun in planning for retirement. As a retiree who has been frugal with his/her incoming money to amass a large retirement nest-egg, you now have the opportunity to use the other side of the personal finance opportunity - let it accumulate and grow as the same compounding effect now adds to your income side year after year. That's the beauty of compound interest. Not to pay today's debt to satisfy your wants. Since most debt that you take money from to pay this special want is not tax deductible, in effect you have to earn $1.00 or more to pay for the dollar and tax of the item you charge. That just screams financial illiteracy. High carrying cost debt makes it easier to postpone meeting your financial goals, and harder to eliminate consumer debt, which serves as a hindrance to achieving financial independence.

Strategies for a Comfortable Retirement

Not all of us want to, are able to, or can maintain our careers into our sixties and seventies. I personally hate to contemplate working in my seventies while managing a tenured law faculty of octogenarians. So, there are other things that we can do to guarantee our quality of life in our retirements. The goal of this book is not necessarily retirement, but certainly comfort in retirement. The strategies in these next pages can be especially useful for bridging the transition in our lives. During the years of building careers and nurturing children, retirement and old age can seem as far off or perhaps unwanted as a distant planet. Then, suddenly, we look at ourselves and ask whether we are ready for the transition that is coming in just a few years or even months.

In the first part of this chapter, I suggested that it is difficult for most of us to have much enjoyment in our older years if we rely on our friends, children, or government to provide for us. Consequently, many of us believe that we will work at least into our sixties and maybe even into our seventies to provide for that phase of our lives when we are less prosperous. In our society, there is a widespread fear of outliving our retirement resources. Social security and pension trouble as well as stories of older people getting by on cat food or barely able to afford the medical care that they need exacerbate the fear.

Managing Finances in Retirement

Seventy-two percent of retirees felt that using professional advice for spending guidance decisions was worthwhile, and 18 percent regretted not having used professional advice. Six out of ten retired individuals rated their spending guidance decision as more important than their monetary planning decision.

People aged 35 to 49 imagined a spending guidance decision as resulting from retirement and found it more difficult to make than current retirees (34 percent vs. 24 percent). In addition to working with a certified financial planner, retired individuals had used other services such as the Foundation for Personal Financial Education (25 percent), mutual funds (29 percent), and companies that offer retirement income planning guidance (24 percent) in preparation. A surprising number had not (11 percent, 7 percent, and 8 percent respectively).

At the instigation of the Charles Schwab Corporation, the Center for Survey Research at the University of Massachusetts conducted a study on spending habits and opportunities for retired individuals.

Once you have retired, adapting to a more constrained cash flow means you need to ensure you do not outlive your resources. Most people will find they have less expendable income after retirement than they enjoyed while working. To ensure a secure and independent existence, it is crucial to prepare for a cessation of earned income by reducing spending. It is much better to gradually reduce spending than suddenly be thrown into circumstances in which you have to do so.

CHAPTER 18

Crisis Management and Financial Resilience

Preparation for crisis management is an evolution, not a fixed state, because our understanding of risk and our preparedness to deal with them change. Unfortunately, you must also find balance between your ability to withstand and recover from crises and not live a terrified, hedged existence. The best way to reduce, but not eliminate, fear is to have maxims. A maxim is a brief statement or a rule of conduct. Keep it simple and easy to remember and duplicate. You want simplicity so that the least intelligent employee can make the right decision in a crisis. You want memorability so that, even when under stress, they won't forget the maxim or abandon the solution. Small teams, easy decisions, and the reinforcement of precious assets – you and your family – will enable safe and quick decision making and help your business and your assets survive a crisis and respond better when it's over.

Crisis management is the art of making swift decisions when bad things happen. It is the ability to avoid getting knocked off course by a hidden rock or a hurricane and knows that the storm won't last forever. Crisis management is your ability to swiftly and confidently protect your freedom, security, and stability when the unexpected happens. You no longer fear crises because you and your assets are strong enough to bounce back – usually better than before. Like your family, you must constantly plan and drill to prepare for the unexpected. Successful plans for crisis management are not just cool black binders full of complex, intricate, and beautiful charts and procedures. They contain the intelligence and skill required to execute your plan for surviving crises and solving your problems.

Preparing for Financial Emergencies

The amount of cash reserves depends on the level of certainty regarding future sources and use of cash flow. Those who receive a fixed income or a salary and have no potential employment problems or disability benefits may select a lower reserve. In contrast, a laid-off factory worker or a self-employed surgeon with the possibility of having $100,000 denials of payment from insurance companies may prefer to carry the higher reserve. It is also appropriate to keep a larger cash reserve with increasing uncertainty. A retired person may need a larger reserve as the tax deadline approaches in case he will owe additional tax, while another retiree may receive a pension statement in January showing a sudden unexpected reduction in his monthly pension benefit. Banks usually offer low-interest checking and savings accounts that provide easy access to the funds. The downside of depositing money in bank accounts is the low return. However, the main purpose of the cash reserves is to ensure emergency access to money when needed.

One of the primary goals of personal financial planning is to limit the possibility of an emergency causing a severe financial crisis. The first step in preparing for an emergency is to avoid them through proper behavior. This includes following traffic laws, maintaining a healthful diet, exercising regularly, using a preventive safety-conscious approach to household management, and seeking routine health care and routine auto maintenance. To further prepare for an emergency, cash reserves should equal two to six months of regular living expenses, depending on a person's particular circumstances. Residents at a higher level of wealth need to prepare for higher potential emergency expenses.

Building Resilience in Times of Crisis

In practical terms, building resilience means considering the financial risks and uncertainties we all face, and planning accordingly. In a financial context, this means a focus on stability, security and liquidity as well as return. A financial plan designed to improve financial resilience is (at least) part of everyone's financial journey. But the strategies to achieve financial resilience are predicated on the way we manage our liquid assets and short-term debt, and how we manage our financial lives over longer time frames, through employment and insurance. By integrating them within our long-term financial plan to build wealth and keep it, we can protect ourselves from the short-term vicissitudes of life, practical and financial, that occur on the way.

What do you do when your grip on financial freedom falters, your dream of early retirement is interrupted by unexpected life events - job loss, serious illness, financial setbacks - or the economy as a whole looks unstable? Like any plan, a financial plan that ignores external risks and assumes a smooth, predictable journey through the years is, at best, a whimsical blueprint. As unwelcome as it may be to contemplate the kind of setbacks and hardships that most of us have suffered at some point, bolstering the resilience of our finances is essential if we are to maintain our focus on long-term progress towards reaching our personal and financial goals. In fact, just as in investment, resiliency is essential to long-term financial viability. By insulating yourself from catastrophic financial shocks, you will be in a more powerful position to invest in assets that are riskier but have greater potential for return.

CHAPTER 19

Social Responsibility and Philanthropy

Most of us like to be philanthropic, and it is easy to be so. Not many people give what they could afford to give. Most feel that if they have more, they can spend more. Spend more you will, but it does not make a person happy. Indeed, anyone involved in friendships, philanthropy, religion, and spirit where emotional wealth is measured differently from financial wealth will be a much happier person than one obsessed with money.

The final stage in the building, preserving, and transfer of wealth is one of giving back. Giving in large amounts only becomes an issue in estate planning or speaking of estates in excess of $50 million. At this point, all the elements have been used - GRATS, FLPs, holding period for assets, etc. And now the time may be at hand to make some substantial contribution to one's favorite charitable organization, university, or hospital. There are many ways to give. The cost in estate taxes of giving can be less than the benefit the charity receives, so once again a win-win-win is possible.

Giving Back to the Community

We are not speaking of those despicable human beings who undertake to perform charitable deeds because they are motivated by the possibility of receiving public acclaim. We are speaking of those individuals who perform good deeds because they feel that performing good deeds is in and of itself worthwhile and fulfilling. Fortune smiled upon them, and they feel that the process of becoming successful and the rewards that accrue with financial success have made their lives meaningful and complete. This feeling makes many wealthy individuals feel that they want to donate their money to help fund the good deeds and noble activities that improve the quality of their community.

Many individuals who have achieved a level of financial freedom contribute to their local community. They do so because they feel that they want to give something back to the community that helped to make them successful. Another reason why some wealthy individuals choose to make a significant contribution to their community is because they believe that by making a contribution to their community, they are not only making their community a better place for its inhabitants but they are also setting a positive example for the other inhabitants of their community. That example is the example of giving back, of social consciousness, and of gratitude for what they have achieved in their lives.

Strategies for Effective Philanthropy

Philanthropy can take many forms. For example, individuals can contribute to charitable causes on a one-time or ongoing basis. They can be hands-on in their philanthropy by contributing their time and skills directly to the organization in which they are interested. Philanthropy often involves giving gifts as part of a natural response to a civic need, a belief in the value of certain causes, or a desire to make a positive contribution to society. Many concepts of philanthropy are fundamental to a concern for the common good. People do not need to be wealthy to be philanthropic. There is no specific latitude of income that defines who can participate in philanthropy, but those who do choose to contribute do so in varying amounts, both large and small. If the intention is to engage in a long-lasting pattern of giving, they often plan their gifts in a way that makes sense in relation to their financial resources.

Engaging in philanthropy can be a rewarding experience and result in considerable personal satisfaction. However, finding the right charitable activities to support can be challenging because you want your contribution to be effective and spent wisely. Think about the kinds of programs and non-profit organizations you enjoy. Philanthropy can include giving money, or it can be more direct, volunteering your time and energy in your community.

CHAPTER 20

Global Perspectives on Financial Freedom

By contrast, for the British, the Dutch, the Swiss, the Australians, and the New Zealanders, the means of attaining financial freedom that they can most readily control are their own homes. Home ownership has been a national priority in all of these countries during the post-World War II era, and government programs have been used to foster individual and family savings to achieve this goal. Indeed, all of Western Europe, as well as the United Kingdom, Canada, Japan, the United States, Australia, New Zealand, and the wealthy South American countries, have very high rates of home ownership. The wealthy South American people in Ecuador, Chile, Jamaica, the Bahamas, Nicaragua, Tunisia, Egypt, and virtually every other country where there is any significant property that exists will primarily invest in their own homes and in their own businesses or farms. In a few special instances, such as the Ifugao in the Philippines, people have made business investments in rice terraces a few days' walk away from their homes. But if you read the National Geographic on a regular basis, you know that this practice, although interesting, is an exception that proves the rule.

Financial freedom is a fundamental human right - the right to free speech carries the right to spend, the right to avoid self-incrimination carries freedom from having wealth seized, and the right to equal treatment carries freedom from coercion, harassment, fines, and intrusive audits. As such, it should be fostered globally. However, different cultures and societies have different perspectives on many things, and financial freedom and security are no exceptions. For example, Americans have very different attitudes about work, money, and investing from many other world cultures.

Cultural Differences in Wealth Building

In fact, while studies clearly demonstrate the disparity in income and wealth among a variety of ethnic backgrounds, they also show a significant pool of economic success among the Asian Indian and Asian Pacific Islander groups. In general, Asian Americans are better educated and have larger incomes than the U.S. average. This is not a new phenomenon: Chinese, Japanese, and Filipino immigrants who arrived in 1900 were typically middle class. Korean immigrants arrived impulse for reform, or from innovative ethnic networks. So it would seem clear that other cultures have some powerful survival lessons that would be helpful for people of all cultures to incorporate in their personal financial management.

A blind spot common among persons from white middle-class backgrounds is the range of distinctions among persons of other cultural backgrounds. A common belief is that minorities within the United States are less financially well-off than the populace as a whole. While the statistics overwhelmingly support this view, the mistake is in assuming that all minority groups are nonwhite and that all nonwhites are economically desperate.

International Investment Opportunities

However, the international investment opportunities are significant. The U.S. companies that dominate overseas markets should capture much of the growth in those markets; foreign firms generally provide additional market share growth opportunities while providing global portfolio diversification. Direct investments in international markets, if conducted carefully, can offer growth and currency gains.

Many of the world's most promising investments are not traded on U.S. regulated exchanges. Foreign markets provide a number of investment opportunities, such as direct investment in international companies, emerging market country funds, U.S. corporations with a significant presence in international markets, foreign currency deposits, and the sudden death of a wage earner is always difficult, but in the case of the battered spouse, the trauma can be even more overwhelming. The couple's funds and other investments held abroad. But in most markets, the cost of the bank negligence insurance, as well as many currency fluctuations, were discussed. In some cases, the risk of an uncertain home for the funds should undermine any global opportunities. Emergency fund managers' attempts at diversification.

CHAPTER 21

Technological Innovations in Finance

However, the processes of creation, transmission, and acceptance of innovations are now taking place at an accelerating pace. In financial markets, the effects of innovations can be fast, where the models, design, and implementation of these technologies can have effects on financial market structure that are not completely understood, sustaining the competitiveness of companies, financial intermediaries, capital markets, and the ability of countries to attract investment. This chapter will examine some of the recent breakthroughs in the application of technology to financial markets, the challenges and risks presented by the increasing implementation of these innovations in practice, and ways by which society can benefit.

The evolution of technology looks set to continue and should enable even greater improvements in the allocation of societal resources. In turn, finance will continue to innovate to provide the required investment to the public that benefits from these technological advances. Innovations direct funds to investments that are expected to provide the most benefit to society. Risk and uncertainty are reduced; information is more efficiently utilized, and market operations become faster, cheaper, and more transparent. Innovations are of existential importance for capital markets. The implementation of new technologies contributes to the growth of a country's economy.

Fintech and Financial Inclusion

The events leading to broader booming changes the story arc. Technology can help achieve an old outcome, such as the promise of financial inclusion, when its time has come. Indeed, there is little new under the fintech sun, and this is a distinction from the AI/ML/dataset boom. The "bits of paper" - building public order around large-scale, face-to-face reconciliation of most trade by the end of the day - is neither a completely new construct (Biometrica, the Chinese Song Dynasty nascent social security system) nor a blockchain system fully deployed (cost of thirteen withdrawals from limited-purpose savings to Chipknip user accounts, when it reached 38 million in the Netherlands, and did subsequently become a full-blown payments system).

We define fintech evolution broadly, combining advances in IT and financial services, and tracing fintech origins to the 18th century. Financial inclusion is the achievement of financial gains enabled via secured, networked virtual access available to all local and global people or organizations. After discussing "traditional observers" who recognize fintech impacts, we examine the experiences of developing countries to explore initial developments needed and the final payment. A challenge is to hold "the bits of paper," building on blockchain research, guiding participants toward the promise of "financial gains in all families, in all cities."

Cryptocurrency and Blockchain Technology

Blockchain is revolutionary. It is as historically important as the rise of the internet itself. A way to describe the magnitude of the importance of blockchain technology is to take someone back to 1993. Everyone was using the postal service or UPS to mail their bills. Amazon and GEICO did not exist. The government put huge and ridiculous age checks on developing what would eventually become the foundation for retail and insurance. If you believed that the speed, safety, and transaction costs of the internet were going to change all of this soon, what would you invest in? The blockchain is the 1993 internet, and you are looking at where the blockchain is about to bring us. The internet might have completely changed our lives, but it seems as if blockchain technology will do an even better job. The speed and cost at which transactions occur on the blockchain are going to flip current financial institutions, the global monetary system, and the retail market on their collective heads. The nascent stage of this technology presents an opportunity of an investment lifetime. As an investor, you should allocate a certain portion of your portfolio to stocks that can profit from the implementation of blockchain technology.

There are a few places you can put your money to achieve what could be life-changing gains. One of these is in the cryptocurrency market. There are over 2,000 different cryptocurrencies, and although the market has lost over 80% of its value from its peak in late 2017/2018, this market is about to change the way money is dealt with. Many financial gurus have called for Bitcoin to reach $100,000 by as soon as 2022. A meager investment can turn into a fortune. You also do not need a lot of money to get into the cryptocurrency market. You can put in $35 and try your luck in this market. Remember, this is an extremely volatile speculative market! Even though ensuring volatility is a cornerstone of any sound financial plan, you have to be careful with this asset class.

CHAPTER 22

Ethics and Values in Wealth Building

In face of these fallacies and in the biggest effort to achieve the pillars of wealth that we want to develop, we analyze the role that ethics and values play in the paths to wealth. We will discuss the part of the ethical principles that must be present in wealth building. We propose that society needs financial independence, guided by a change of values represented by mindfulness and the development of a prospering society. These ethical pillars built into capitalists contribute to the creation of a wealth that is clean and, as we pursue them, open for us to forests of hope, respect, dignity, and improved quality of existence. Our thoughts are of change, of awareness, of change actions. Our manifest of wisdom for the wealth and value that will guide the actions of these civilizing entrepreneurs of ethics are provided in the last section of the chapter.

There was a time in history when wealth was considered a blessing from heaven or a fortunate gift. Over the years, the Protestant Ethic has helped to debunk such mistaken ethical concepts that the rich had achieved their status through divine favor. Nevertheless, over the years the cinema and some politicians, the advertising media and some leaders, have tried everything possible to dim the light of wisdom and the earnestness of the poor in humble origins by sabbatogenetic displays. You know, in the broad reaches of Brazil and the many other economically unequal countries, the masses think that wealth is originally hollow, hollow, hollow in origin, soiled and black, and that lies, usually, must refer to its maturation. Because of greed, a bunch of moneylenders have formed to grow rich by working (or not working) at the expense of devotees and religious poor.

Ethical Investing Practices

Socially responsible investment aims at creating added social value both in the short and long run. Investing ethically is not just a blend of pure and abstract ethical considerations. Their practical application can generate operating advantages for the companies reviewed and their financial backers. The goal is to invest in companies adopting effective social, environmental, and social sustainability policies, aware that some investment themes may have such vastly different investment return profiles as to create a conflict between ethical values and expected return.

Ethical investing relies on a series of practices that seek to apply to capital the principles of sustainable development, corporate social responsibility, or the fulfillment of particular ethical objectives. This can often lead to the pursuit not only of strictly shareholder-based objectives, but also of goals involving investment in the overall satisfaction of human needs or in the encouragement and reinforcement of respect for human rights. An ethical investor can, for example, agree with the goal of earning a return but refuse to invest in the shares of companies dealing in controversial sectors and seek instead opportunities for positive investing - for those companies aiming to create added social or environmental value in the short and long run while respecting ethical principles as much as possible.

Aligning Wealth with Values

What went wrong? Clearly, more than money is required to lead a satisfied life. If we aspire to financial freedom, freedom over our time and what we wish to do with it, we don't want to end up proper rich and poor, in spiritual agony over what we did to get there. Instead, framing our decisions in the context of our own life goals, family's values, and the positive impact that we can make on the world for good can increase the meaning and joy of life, promote mental health, often reduce the amount of wealth required to retire, add passion to spending, and help ensure that each step that we take, each choice that we make reflects who we are rather than who we would like to be.

So on we worked and waited for the light, And went without the meat, and cursed the bread; And Richard Cory, one calm summer night, Went home and put a bullet through his head.

And he was rich, rich - yes, richer than a king - And admirably schooled in every grace: In fine, we thought that he was everything To make us wish that we were in his place.

And he was always quietly arrayed, And he was always human when he talked; But still he fluttered pulses when he said, "Good morning" and he glittered when he walked.

Whenever Richard Cory went downtown, We people on the pavement looked at him: He was a gentleman from sole to crown, Clean favored and imperially slim.

Why is it important to examine values as part of our strategies for financial success? This is critically important because increasingly many individuals are concluding that money is never enough. The poem "Richard Cory" by Edwin Arlington Robinson describes a millionaire who seemingly has it all:

CHAPTER 23

Conclusion and Key Takeaways

The first step towards financial freedom involves defining your goals. As simple as it may sound, it has been well-documented that most individuals have only a vague idea of the items they desire to achieve from a financial standpoint, and few articulate any tangible goals or a financial plan. After an individual fully understands his goals, the most successful approach is to save and invest in such a manner that a diversified wealth-building program is created. Successful building of wealth requires careful implementation of a disciplined savings plan, with attention paid to preserving hard-earned capital. By thinking long-term, seeking out opportunities that are rooted in the success of the underlying company, and most importantly, examining the wealth-building program on a risk-adjusted basis, investors can successfully build their financial freedom.

The quest for financial freedom lies deep within the American spirit. It is a firm belief that in order for America to succeed, it must embody freedom in all aspects of our lives, with financial freedom included as a fundamental cornerstone. The opportunities for growth and self-fulfillment which a lifestyle of freedom enables are worthy of pursuit. The financial freedom journey is replete with trade-offs and personal choices. These will almost always require difficult decisions and nearly always require extended periods of time to accomplish. However, throughout history, it has been shown that wise, disciplined choices, along with the passage of time, are a few of the key cornerstones necessary for rising above mediocrity and achieving a successful outcome.

Summary of Strategies and Principles

Five basic principles of investing in financial assets are: that the objective of financial investment is to achieve real growth of wealth; that individuals should invest primarily in productive assets that produce real goods and services, such as business companies, unit trusts or common stock; that productive real assets should be acquired to match the time horizons of the investors; that the obvious constraint on the acquisition of productive assets is the ready availability of debt capital; and that the activities of young, well-financed investors in new securities with strong growth potential are likely to be more successful since they are not yet burdened with past mistakes.

The objective of a sound financial plan is to maximize the return to the owner of wealth over the long run. The key to the effective management of financial wealth is adherence to a few basic principles and use of appropriate financial strategies. The investment principles on which the strategies are based are essentially those which professional investment counselors follow in advising their clients. Finesse - the art of negotiating financial-market transactions in your own best interest - can also have a substantial impact on wealth. Finally, a word about wealth counseling: many individuals prefer to construct personal financial planning based only on the basic principles; such a course, involving simple implementation, can be highly effective in personal management of financial wealth.

Next Steps for Achieving Financial Freedom

Visualize the money mountain top. Setting your financial course is like climbing a mountain; the peak of the mountain represents the first day of your financial freedom. Take a piece of paper, draw a mountain, and mark an X at the top. If you know your exact goal in terms of dollars, print it by the X. If you don't know how much money will be enough, because you're unclear about what you want, then print the word "freedom" by that X. All you may need to do is to eliminate your debt and your confusion will be completely gone. All of your money-related decisions will be obvious, easy to make, and will result in personal freedom. At this point, you will be glad you took the time to come up with the appropriate dollar amount of that X at the top of your mountain.

Before you begin, to be successful at making and following through on financial plans, you should learn to become passionate about the subject of money. How does one become passionate about money? By visualizing and then putting to use the financial freedom that you will have in the future. Imagine finally having free time to do what you want, when you want, and with whom you want to do it. Keep visualizing these mountain tops of the mind until you achieve the intense desire that goes along with the passion for financial freedom. Also, make educating yourself about the world of money part of that pursuit and the passion will grow.

When to start? There's no specific age at which you should begin working toward financial freedom, but many people begin this lifelong journey as soon as they begin working. The earlier you begin, the easier it will be. Some people don't begin until they start a family and realize that they have to provide for others as well. Starting later in life doesn't mean that financial freedom won't be possible, but you'll need to make larger contributions to your plans in order to make up for lost time.

www.ingramcontent.com/pod-product-compliance
Lightning Source LLC
LaVergne TN
LVHW090328210926
848480LV00004B/1336